WHIRLING

By the same author:

The Amorous Cannibal (1985)
I'm Deadly Serious (1988)
For Crying Out Loud (1990)
Rungs of Time (1993)
Selected Poems 1956–1994 (1995, 1997)

CHRIS WALLACE-CRABBE

Whirling

Oxford Melbourne New York
OXFORD UNIVERSITY PRESS
1998

Oxford University Press, Great Clarendon Street, Oxford OX2 6DP

Oxford New York

*Athens Auckland Bangkok Bogota Bombay Buenos Aires
Calcutta Cape Town Dar es Salaam Delhi Florence Hong Kong Istanbul
Karachi Kuala Lumpur Madras Madrid Melbourne Mexico City
Nairobi Paris Singapore Taipei Tokyo Toronto Warsaw*

*and associated companies in
Berlin Ibadan*

Oxford is a trade mark of Oxford University Press

*First published in Oxford Poets
as an Oxford University Press paperback 1998*

*British Library Cataloguing in Publication Data
Data available*

Library of Congress Cataloging in Publication Data
Wallace-Crabbe, Chris.
Whirling / Chris Wallace-Crabbe.
p.   cm. — (Oxford poets)
I. Title.   II. Series.
PR9619.3.W28W47   1998   821—dc21   97–49970
ISBN 0-19-288081-0

1 3 5 7 9 10 8 6 4 2

*Typeset by George Hammond Design
Printed in Great Britain by
Athenæum Press Ltd.
Gateshead, Tyne and Wear*

For David Constantine

From the shadow of the prehistoric world emerge
dying religions that have not yet invented gods or
goddesses, but live by the mystery of the elemental
powers of the Universe, by the complex vitalities of
what we feebly call Nature.

D. H. Lawrence, *Etruscan Places*

ACKNOWLEDGEMENTS

Many of these poems first appeared in the pages of the following journals: *The Age, Antipodes, Brisbane Courier-Mail, Canberra Times, Eureka Street, Harvard Review, Mattoid, Meanjin, Metre, Melbourne University Gazette, Poetry* (Chicago), *Quadrant, RePublica, Salt, Times Literary Supplement, Ulitarra, Verse, Voices,* and *Worcester Review*.

'Don Giovanni' was first published in the programme for a Victorian State Opera's 1996 production of Mozart's masterwork. 'Timber' has appeared as an artist's book produced by Bruno Leti of Melbourne and Raphael Fodde of New York. A number of poems have been heard on the Australian Broadcasting Commission. My thanks are due to all these editors and artists, and to Sonja Chalmers, of the Australian Opera, formerly at the Victorian State Opera, for permission to use this work.

CONTENTS

WHIRLING

SUMMER'S BREATH

At the first real heat, analogies
come skulking round the bend of self,
cicadas trilling like an orchestra
warming up for Rachmaninov,
body drinking its own lassitude
      straight from the fridge.

The world is thick with difference;
pale steamy smog invades you
carrying all the pollens in its knapsack;
and the ever-so-dreamy turtledoves
keep rasping, 'Old Colquhoun, old Colquhoun'
      from their own high wire.

As though your blood clogged up with carbon
or sulphur, rituals attend
the downing and the rising of your nights.
New joints announce themselves in thigh and elbow
while your dreams chug along in second
      like a T-model Ford.

Eye and antrum have gritty messages
they want to exchange; discomfort
knows his way through the family thesaurus.
You're lucky to be alive, a phrase
that contains its personal shadow
      of disbelief.

It is time to keep on quaffing cheap champagne,
perhaps to drop Russell and Rorty for Proust.
Stars go walking all over your body
while ghostly leg-spinners are on at the MCG,
for this heat contains the heat of earlier days
      and will drive you crazy.

WHAT LANES REVEAL

Nameless ways oddly bumbling away by
garage doors, roller or weatherboard,
under Tassie bluegums, pushy jasmine stars,
yellow grenades of lemon, the secular
gesticulation and sprawl of biblical fig;

these cobbles represent the Argument from Design.
Our lives are an archaeology: the green science
of garden-dating, detail-sniffing, hunches
about this back gate connecting with which front,

what brand of superannuated hippy
in tan corduroys with a stunningly tanned girlfriend
lives in that done-up loft.
                              Do mystical students
pad in these upjumped stables, play Segovia,
false on about Krishna, diversify brown rice?
They, even they, can brood over ageing.

The past survives in rust-antique iron surfaces
corrugated from here to kingdom come,
which it probably won't at the end of the century,
a bad end—which is where we happen to be,
stumbling on sprained ankles
                              through imported
holograms of frail reality.

GLORYING

Small things first,
            perception without signals . . .

but look, the mintbush head
        is a frond or quivering crowd
                of purple darkthroated bells

        and white stars with five points
        ride all over the mock-orange,
a gale of jasmine springtime fuddling us all,
            much like infantile perversity.

I don't believe that misery can be
    quite so brightly coloured
                        as happiness,
        at least not
        on this cloudmarbled planet,
        this highly unlikely stage
        for consciousness to prop and flutter.

        Still, here we are
        and below their windflicked green
                    fistfuls of cardiac leafage
        the fuchsia flowers are all still dangling down,
        descendants of a nailed and bleeding god
            or lipstick-hued corps-de-ballet;

but sweep it all aside
                for now
        moving forward into freedom
        by the pure saying-so.

'There is no Europe,' hum the endless trees
dancing on tiptoe, frothy clouds of chlorophyll,
'the truly strong will reinvent Australia,
like innocence.'
And we sense, under the whirligig of stars,
some edge of time is ripe:
high noon,
blue oceanic factories,
buckets of banksia-cones.

TIMBER

When the pearly rain
    comes pelting in at this angle
and the dark stringybark branches
    look brittle and dangerous
you roundly un-Heathcliff yourself
    so as to head
        for creature comforts.

    And then the question rises:
could there be
    a book that really would
set everything at ease?
    Even the Holy Bible
hasn't managed it yet
    not even on its better days
        long before the martyrs.

What is it
    that other people do?
Could they describe
    the taste of spring water
evocatively?
    And we do have to wonder
in whose fluent mind
        history gets made,
embryonically.

Like most of you
    I'm obliged to say
        that it wasn't me,
not for worlds.

II

Against the blue, against the whatsoever,
a tower of poplar has been lashing away
like damaged birds.

Some blown demon has to invade my life,
shorting all the circadian rhythms
and buffeting me aside.

Body inhabits a throbbing
or some vice-versa, crudely at odds with time.
Is a brainstorm plus or minus?

The eastward sky behind that heaving tree
is dirty pearls.
                    Nothing short
of a cold whalebreath of wind
skirls in from chaos,
turning personality outside in.

Nowhere is everywhere by now.

III

The tousled children
have their own way
                    with trees,
their own classification:

How is this one to climb?
Are the branches convenient?
What about splinters and thorns?

Their aim
a perfect lookout
                    or lofted cubby-house
in dense leafage,

close to the old gods.

In boyhood, there was fascination with mallee roots,
no objects on our planet
were less geometrical. They were
the purely organic, naturally baroque.

Yet in a neighbouring woodyard they were stacked
in an enormous cube,
a solid brown rick
of culture working on still life.

We bought them. Just a few.

And they burned for us.

V

A dark season lurked
        in the middle of that summer;
I laboured with pen
        and pencil, axe and hammer.

While chopping on the slope
        I cracked a short log open
and saw a glossy cricket
        squat on the wood, unshaken;

at first he would not budge:
        when I came back he had gone,
had crawled off into dry grass
        and summer's heat came on.

VI

Lingered smell of Scotch pine,
aromatic as a bunch of lavender,
stars bursting through the jagged branches
and little tags of resin
        sticky on both my hands.

The shouldering ash-tree,
close, greenfeathery, witch-encumbered,
was felled at eleven today.

A tree-man shinned slowly up
the living trunk
riding upon spiked boots

or futuristic gaiters.
Big branches came stripping away,
each with a soft crash.

A white snow of nuptial sawdust
lies across the backyard.

The sky can get at us now:
more and more stars in my hair.

Alone, in coffeecoloured twilight
you gravely turn back
to unresponsive others:
granite, water and wood.

Wood is the hand's old friend,
as club, or careworn grip
into a rocking green treetop;
grainy for tool or sport.

Split redgum can cry
splinteringly to the heart
or a whippy branch whistle through air,
the life still in it.

When I smell timber
it flows inside me;
touching its edge, I feel
the coarse flesh of all being;

but in a stand or copse
of windlashed alterity
I might now also hear
the first gods murmuring.

IX

Ebony, balsa, oak, mahogany,
    bo-tree, ti-tree, pepperina,
        red cedar, blackwood, Glastonbury thorn,
    hemlock, mulga, sandalwood, yew . . .

TOUGH TIMES

But hang on, whose city are we living in?
Can buildings truly control behaviour
wishing the people had only one head?
There's egg on the information superhighway,
resilience in local culture
and a limestone dream of Italian regions,
too rich and subtle for the petrified tourist.
(The Tiber flowing through travertine.)

Will space be truer full, or empty,
given that nature abhors a city
while a medley of moccasins and yuppies
takes the flight into purity and suburbia?
The erotics of shopping will bring back frocks,
old electronic ware, short white views,
and the knowledge that he who despises himself
esteems himself as a self-despiser.

We yearn for a hamlet on the Ganges
or the woolly green land of motionless childhood
while the usual dickhead political thugs
control our state in the usual way.

Licking the marmalade off our fingers
might be the limit of what we do,
timid souls,
                    given to self-expression
like fluffed-out pussycats.

The Yarra flowing through yellow sandstone
listens to us not wanting to die:
stuck in the parrot-riddled suburbs
we might as well study nature
                    because it is very old
and because the bark peels off. Hang on.

WANTING TO BE A SCULPTOR

to make iron grow like a tree
to discover truths in Huon pine
or compete with the loveliness of river pebbles
to invent a ceramic language
to encourage silver and brass to dance
                articulating air
to hack slowly into redgum
even to find a poise for plastic bags
        and mineral water bottles
to find great stones
and stand them incongruously upright
on some hill or in a large paddock
        making a sort of shrine there
to gather a jumble of bits and pieces
turning it into a true occasion of beauty
                ranged in modern space

        that would be the shot

THE WHISTLE STOP

I heard a bloke whistling the other month
and wondered what on earth had become of whistling.
People used to do it a lot of the time.
Everyone except me could whistle in tune,
well, that was what it felt like back in the forties;
but, human history being the way it seems to be,
everything rolls away: the ice-chest, milkmen's horses,
Hypol, the place kick, dicky-seats, and our youth.
Maybe a lot of people whistle secretly
or else it gets done between consenting adults
in a private apartment over glasses of sherry.
It's easy to interpret things wishfully
but maybe whistling has simply up and gone west
like being able to pull the sword from a stone.

AN EQUINE PROSPECT

Some undistinguished evening,
tooling along out back of Woop Woop
you see them all of a sudden,
two glossy horses
fingered by the late sun's copper rays.
They might have been here for ever,
one bleachy-white, one chestnut, both
romantic and melancholy.
Weeds rustle, redgums doze
                tall across the macadam,
but these two horses remain
with all the nobility
of cycladic figures:
                austere, pure, taut.

Nothing in their dignity could ever
hint that for several millennia
they've allowed themselves to fall
into servitude, or village symbiosis:
whether as cavalry-thud,
dragging double-buggies up tan dirt roads
or persuading Missy to hold her seat
                long before the gymkhana.

Puff-clouds turn pale orange,
the shadows have stretched like gymnasts
and the horses remain
complete in their upright musculature.

                Goodbye, proud nags.

We thrum over the ridge towards tonight
and they have slid away
like the fossil memory
                of diminutive eohippus
trotting through ferns briskly
and the oiled olympian gods.

GLITTER

The common mind is a winter palace:
it gleams a lot with gold and mirrors,
delights in complicated parquetry,
can turn as green as malachite,
hang out elaborate candelabra
or celebrate the dead in beaten silver.

It plays with lust and luxury,
and if it should come to know
that somewhere out on the pitch-dark river
there bobs a grey cruiser
whose guns will smash
all that coruscating artifice—
glass, porphyry, jasper, gilt—
why, it will only delight the more
in furniture and fantasy.

Mind will not mind at all;
it leaps the more it comes to know
all we delight or glory in
stands on a dull bank of the darkening river.

St Petersburg

SAMARKAND

Thin golden smell: Uzbekistan,
starlight on the heavenly domes,
the drift of Asia through my hair.

Here, distrait, dwindled between
the marvellous madrassehs
I felt the peace which Islam does not seem

to give in life. There in the cobbled court—
bloody enough once, or more than once—
I felt the planets lean down and touch

the ground beside me
like cogs in a gigantic silence.
Cats lope across the lanes

and the trees this year
are bearing a heavy crop of choughs.
This folded silk-town flies from Russia

into its own place, into
Tamburlaine's goldstarred mausoleum
under that blue dome

which is not a breast
but, segmented like an orange,
the very sky come down to rest.

So from this air as dry as cat-fur
the stars go swimming through my blood
mouthing Asia,
                        Asia,
                                    Asia.

PLACE NAMES: THE NAME

Fauve Collioure.
                      Remember the pike terrine at Collioure?
At Sommières we slept in a high, riverside carpet mill;
Carcassonne had been a disneyfied folly of Viollet-le-duc;
I'll be coming back to Salazac (accidental rhyme) later on;
we missed out completely on Arles and the Alyscamps
but toodled up the Rhone after calling on friends
and then took a right to mountain-ringed Grenoble,
the city Stendhal adored not to be in at all—
he who thought Italian ice cream so delicious
that somebody ought to have banned it from the start;
at Chambéry we lodged at the cutest little inn
and bought some nice shirts, or could they have been jerseys?
We were lucky not to spend much time in Geneva
but the Swiss belong in another, probably smaller poem.
So we got back to Salazac and all the fun of the farm,
including our foolhardy fight with a randy young stallion;
got pissed with hippies down at Holy Ghost Bridge
and played tennis on the very lip of the Ardêche Gorge
above shaggy limestone, canoes and neolithic caves,
or went off shopping in modern Bagnols-sur-Cèze.
As merry as bluebirds we drank beaume-de-venise
in the agreeable environs of streamthreaded Goudargues;
marvelled at the workaholic Romans' Pont du Gard;
drove down to Avignon for the disappointed bridge
and to Orange for a theatre's great bones.
(So many things in Europe seem to be orange
or used to be; very few are called Lemon.)
But I can't rabbit on for ever and it's high time
that I mentioned Paris, just like everyone else,
with its kickshaws, bouquets, flics and *je ne sais quoi*,
all so poetic I couldn't write poetry there
but lay in bed with the bulgy mumps instead,
looking out at planeleaves from the Grand Hôtel de Lima.
On the way back north we took a hopeful squizzy
at the drizzling, commercial, unProustian beach of Cabourg.

18

THE IDEA OF MEMORY AT 33 CELSIUS

Who then is it speaking through me
in shorts and T-shirt, padding at ease
over the faintly dusty floorboards,
while a shining universe
remembers time as the field of deeds,
readily available somehow?

We lay hold of the world in miniature,
so far, so blue, so calm that now
it appears like a snow-crystal,
quaintly colourful on the mantelpiece
while summer roars along outside
in a heady perfume of eucalyptus.

Lendl said that after a match
he could remember every stroke.
I'll take that with a pillar of salt.

On the other hand, memory would seem to be
a dovecot with birds in pigeonholes,
painted grey by original sin
or perforated like a colander
with icecold water pouring through it
and running away
down the pipe forever.

Are we able to get a grip
on the disappearing universe . . .
                    There's a big ask

                                  for dear life
in the heart of cicada weather.

ONE LIFE, OR MANY

Under the circumstances
oddly flowing, a metamorphic self
drains into guttering moments, pools
in the mudsoft gully.
Reinvention
stands up a little row
of cardboard identities, frail
on the folding table—
the old kind, with shaky legs.
You are the vulnerable Jack of Clubs.

The stream bends,
fanning round a log
doing ripple-patterns of great
immediate subtlety, graphic seductiveness.
Blue-glinting dragonflies
glide through the moment
in which you stoopingly exist
as a hatless observer of nature
in her spring-fed prime.
Oddly flowing
in the old way,
light blushes the crown of a gum sapling
taking part in a green world
which the present has grown out of,
or away from . . .

You close your book
and groan another modern groan,
stiff in the hams, mosquito-brushing
but still romantic
as moonlight. That is the way
the cards have fallen for you now:
they are part of something larger, by far.

ERSTWHILE

Your girlfriend rang me up today,
your former girlfriend,
                              no, that isn't right,
the present friend of all that once was you,
your fetch or
what remains in the little photographs:
a boy in black-and-white
riding a horse into the scrub
or, freckled, reading out of doors,
both times T-shirted,
your hair a thick, dark bowl-cut,
                              my erstwhile son.

Oh yes, she rang today,
had taken somebody out to see your grave
near the forked white trunk,
and we were sad together
on the phone, for a hard while
thinking of you, long gone now. Hence.
Where? Where are you?
In poor fact I can never come to grasp
the meaning of it all, supposing
that to be what religion's all about.
The loss remains behind
                              like never being well.

FLOROBIOGRAPHY

At first,
leaving aside the lairy purple of garage morning glories,
it was nasturtiums that spoke of colour
and I boldly chewed their leaves,
walking along the brick edge of a gardenbed,
to please a little girl called Jill.

Then it was bulbs
in a sandy springtime
bursting alight under the edge of apple-trees,
breaking the green with
the different characters of
jonquil, grape hyacinth and freesia.

Buddleia trumpets
dangled their flopping creamy-white
through my perfectly undistinguished
teenagerhood:
they were nothing special, except for the bees.

In the northern hemisphere
with its overstated seasons
I came in time to meet
the daffodil and crocus
of European literature,
treating them as if they were nightingales.

Pepper-and-salt years
of empirical observation
taught me to feather like a parrot
at all the teasing varieties
of hairy gum-tree blossom,
through summers of my discontent

with the universe itself,
loving the parts of it, though, little by little,
as the beak of an eastern spinebill goes into the hakea.

GRANDFATHER

Arriving like a smoked salmon
in sprawling Adelaide

he met this ever-so
fiery little blonde from Cork,

a real Cluny Macpherson
escaping the sweaty kisses of cattle kings.

He turned on the macho charm
like Arbroath brose,

snapped her up,
forgot his children far away in Cheshire

and metamorphosed into a Highlander
with a moustache

as thick
as the birks of Aberfeldy.

His diamond mine in seductive Queensland
was not cut out to make it

and like us all
he died in the end,

but long before I was thought of.

MEMORIES OF VIN BUCKLEY,
SPELT FROM SIBYL'S GOLDEN LEAVES

This elegant autumn weather
filling goldcoined Grattan Street
brings you obliquely back again,
small-footed, huffing along to Martini's
        rather slowly
toward grilled whiting   gradual white wine,
your bag full of serious minor complaints
against the universe.

'Now piss off, mate,' you said to a classic bore,
with all the gallantry of a dauphin.
        You rendered unto Caesar
the shit that was Caesar's, wittily;
when in form, you really could be
as flash as a rat with a gold tooth
or a courteous falcon.
        Dear old friend, you thought
the sexy falcons in 'They Flee from Me'
just might have been racehorses.

Your wit was that of the hooded owl,
scrupulously nodding. Once you fell
into the fireplace, dancing with Gwennie
among the aphorisms of claret-purple cronies;
and rose up unscorched, blinking.
        This Maybright weather
is no doubt still trickily playing
on those huge trattoria windows
behind which we sipped and planned
to change the whole face of Australian Lit,
        outwitting the weasel cunning
of dwellers in the great Coathanger's shade,
        harbour-dazzle apparatchiks
and Marxified weanlings.

Yellow, frail, eddied, a linden leaf
                    trails its gyre around me.
Trust nobody but women and old friends,
your ghost would still say,
treading on soundless delicate feet
past all the Celtic takers and mistakers
who had your measure pretty clear,
                    they thought.

THE YEARS

Evan, it's over thirty years,
but does not seem a third so long
since we sat maundering over beers
reciting Trinculo's poignant song.

To Hope and Dickinson and Yeats
we sipped away the setting sun
but Wystan Auden drove the fates
and Marvell crumbled under Donne.

Those little pubs where we played darts
have failed, or fallen back to sod.
Gosh, how romantic were our hearts,
hankering for an absent god

to guarantee the serious
and guide us flaring through the dark.
Remember those delirious
third quarters at Victoria Park

when your great Magpies turned around
a game that looked as bad as lost
to wave on wave of gathered sound:
a rover never counts the cost.

Our children seem what we were then
though drifting at a gentler rate.
We will not reach the source again;
these river-bends are adequate.

Did I say thirty years?
                    It may
seem nothing to eternity
but has proved long enough to play
strange tunes against our memory.

YEARS ON

At the trailing edge of autumn
grey rain is falling hard
to soften the native grasses
in the old graveyard.

My son is tucked well under there
among the clay and stones,
though what his name betokens
is nothing more than bones.

And how long would it take for
the water to soak down
and cover every bone with
its fine, transparent gown?

I do not know, merely recall
moments of pleasure and mirth.
As he trod lightly on you,
rest lightly on him, earth.

WITTGENSTEIN'S SHADE

Dear Gwen,
             I like to believe
that every softened evening
an austere, courteous ghost
comes in glidingly and stands
by your bed or chair,
slowly saying something like
'What God commands, that is good.'

A regular ghost,
he comes in a tweed jacket
and crumpled college slacks,
stands by you, a little stiffly,
murmuring something pretty much like
'Sound doctrines are all useless.'

I think he comes
             like a stray bird
in through your blown curtains
with his pained, patrician face,
his accent of gone Vienna,
offering you the observation:
'the river-bed of thoughts may shift.'

You are further in
that river-bed than I am;
he returns from the other side.
His mouth has been drawn
as tight as the skin on a drum,
yet he seems quite as innocent as
the breast-feathers of a dove
and he tells you, 'It is love
that believes the resurrection.'

He will visit you, day after day.

A THRESHOLD FOR MY SON

You touch the door now, trembling on its hinge
between vague adolescence and the dark
exciting world an adult stumbles in.
(Those are not monsters: they are only gumtrees,
so take it easy.) You are seventeen

and nothing is mysterious about that,
except that all maturing somehow is
a journey through an unmapped, shadowy park:
black trees, bird-cries, lugubrious pond
but nothing you can firmly recognize.

You do not know what teams you're going to play,
nor even what the local rules may be,
but play you must, at times heroically
and yet on other days just getting by:
having enough of the ball to earn your place.

Today I spied an eagle floating slowly
along the ridge, taking a bird's-eye-view
of luck below; it hung at ease
on the blue air; and yet was governed by
a fine-tuned observation of the world;

that's the balance to be striven for,
a difficult strategy, defining life
at the high, blue behest of happiness.
Walk tall, dear son.
                              Go straight ahead in joy
making the grassy landscape all your own.

WE LIVE IN TIME SO LITTLE TIME

But is the harried moment
of diary or digital
the one fabric

with rollover seasons
that recirculate leafage,
colour and dryness?
The same cloth cut longer?

And is it again
the same box-and-dice
as reminiscent decades of simplicity
replayed in micro-cinema:
tooth fairy, wishbone, Easter bunny?

Where do I stand
on the shifting slabs
of glamorous centuries
when things were all different,
cross-gartered, crinolined, with
half-crippled sad oafs lugging
sedan chairs through shit and mud?

Or, poor atom,
blinking among millennia
as the shellfish change into cliffs
with knobbled cave and winding fault?
As the tall peaks abrade?

And a greeting might even be
on its way down here
from souls on another planet
billions of years ago,

slowly eking its path

                              to us
in our fragile future

wherever it is we are,
glinting with desperate hope.

OF FINITE HEARTS THAT YEARN

Latter mid-afternoon:
the dustblue mountains were at rest
on memory's eastern rim
like sheep.

Half a-drowse
one might well have been swimming
in the airy subjunctive
of clouds

with sturdy companions
hauling the logic of girder and joist
after them along
through twirling shallows
and shadow trees,

the whole
adding up
to a picture of consciousness
you couldn't see
because you were a slanting patch
of red and blue, light tan,
etcetera,
lodged inside it.

The flowering-gum
hovered reliably nearby
murmuring like an aunt,
but rich beyond all this there loomed and dangled
the wish to fail:
dark as a raven, always there,
a no-loss situation.

ANTIPODES

Everything under that sky
believes in living
with its golden opposite,

a soothing anima,
the secret sharer,
unblinking social lion
laying them in the aisles,

the undead shadow
breathing ice on your neck
when you least want it,
or even most.

There is a zest
in all alternatives:
everyone is a version
of someone else.

A BARBARIAN CATECHISM

No, dear friend,
I don't have a full heart
for all the Christian stock and barrel, but
with half a mind still need
much of it some of the time, at least until
something more serious
comes along, which hasn't happened yet.
Epiphanies are for real, given
that 'man is not equally moral all the time',
according to clever, dangerous
Nietzsche, who liked to say he was really Polish,
not a goofy German,
and declared that Christianity came along
in order to lighten the heart.

So Christmas is hard to get away from still,
despite the cards and toys,
those haunting carols again and again calling back
our own childhood as well
as His, an absolutely important
child in a wintry manger,
prickly with straw, whether or not he was
the child of God, like us
or seriously different. Yes, he died in the spring,
which was autumn down here in Australia,
but his sacrifice has got muddled with rabbits and eggs.
Again, I am pretty dodgy
about angels and saints, while the life everlasting
is an awesome whatnot which
just keeps on changing utterly all the time.
Grace I can understand;
it would make sense to a perfectly heathen soul
and so might Blessing.
Indeed, lacking Grace, how could we endure
the painfulness of days?

For these, for all the incomparable stories,
  tall articulate churches
and Piero della Francesca's 'Baptism of Christ'
  I give wholeminded thanks
and bless a tradition that sheds a various light
  like stained glass windows
on the stuttering thisness of our here-and-now.

NEAR AREZZO

Golden days to you all.
I was Piero,
the well-mannered, new
painter from Borgo

and my job descriptions
were far from easy to handle:
how on earth do you fit
an important offshore visitor
into the same pictorial space
as Our Lord being whipped and scorned?

I had skill.
I had the tool of perspective.
I set to work in joy,
                and made it.

DON GIOVANNI

Emerging from the mist of Latin Europe
(The heat-haze rather, sensual as paella)
He flourishes his rapier like a you-know-what,
Transforming every day to narrative
Or hyper-tragicomic bedroom stuff.
Of course he's quite as dangerous as music,
Which Plato should have banished from the state,
Its lovely tunes unmanning piety.

Anna's father resurrects in marble;
Ottavio's a dag with lovely songs:
Even a nerd can access plangency,
Especially when in love. It all takes place
At some wonderful tavern of the mind
Where Shakespeare's boozing on with Aeschylus,
Berlioz vamping on an old piano
For Catherine of Siena and Jeanne d'Arc.

The Don's a Lamborghini aristocrat
Who would have had a pad in the Western District
Or Cap Ferrat. He isn't really nice
And yet those ladies have the hots for him:
Their knickers tremble when he just walks by.
The masculine myth is all get up and go,
With an irresponsibility that charms.
(He had a thousand lays in Catholic Spain.)

I'm still not sure who wins out in the end,
Romantic anti-hero or stone ghost,
But it is Big; and the mere survivors
Are numbly free again for daily business,
To go on being virtuous, or nice.
Zerlina knows she has a certain balsam
That's sovereign for bruises and sore heads.

Careful, dear: that's where it all began.

THE CRIMS

What has become of them, those actual gunmen,
    Drily disguising the hurry
In which they live out chaotic combative lives,
    Neither Bogart nor Peter Lorre?

Do they stand in bar-doorway shadow, an overcoat collar
    Fashionably turned up
With shooting iron in a shoulder-holster, just in case
    They have been sold a pup?

Do they slope into some club, confront a slinky blonde
    Poured into strapless black,
A fag adroop from her pouting bee-stung lip,
    Both ignoring some hack

Of a sneering punk posted behind the piano,
    Or does that only happen in books
And in black-and-white films with lots of venetian blinds?
    Plain cooking makes plain cooks

And our actual, workaday crims may well have never
    Frozen through a dissolve.
More likely they're shonky hitmen pushing smack,
    Leaving small puzzles to solve

For patient introverts from the CID
    Or serious cops in a Ford.
They've drifted crimeward because they're faintly clever,
    Lazy, amoral and bored.

A few are names, like Harrison and Bradshaw,
    Trimbole and Taylor (Squizzy)
Who buried his guns in everyone's backyard,
    Keeping our folklore busy.

The rest have dropped with yellowing newspapers
    Into the bin of history.
Couch potatoes, we doze in the 1990s
    Watching some video mystery;

No doubt there are plenty of new hoods all around us,
    Fighting, fucking and cursing—
But in my ballad no reference is intended
    To any living person.

SNIPS OF A DAY
or Flow

What would it be like to write a journal that managed to get everything in, which would flow *and* reach out sideways, forward and back, grasping the small and the large, all that myriad of impressions? Generically, it would have to be some kind of hungry version of Proust or of *Ulysses*; too much causation or temporality would upset the whole apple cart. One needs a genre with appetite, with a huge belly, the kind of caboodle Whitman had to invent for *Leaves of Grass*. Just today, for instance I would like to have got in the dog's expanding leash, my bottle shop conversation with Eddie, foxgloves out in a couple of gardens, the hyperactive supermarket manageress with her high heels clattering frenetically down the aisles, nearly losing my Visa card on the floor at K Mart, chatting with Olly in the deli *re* his exams, Emma with a towel wrapped round her head, Dean Jones's century against Pakistan, Bunuel's *Diary of a Chambermaid*, a blackbird's melodious evensong high in the backyard ash tree, Marianne's call from flash Noosa, Finzi's Hardy songs and why I listen so obsessively to them, Toby's indifference to his maths exam, whether to make a banana cake, the coming heat, my lack of tennis partners, a sentence Peter wrote in *The Age* about Robert Graves (viz., 'Graves' life was notably "tasteless", even for a human being'), my sleepiness during John Clarke's monologues late last night, when to change the bed-clothes, watering the strawberry plants or not, why Jeanne Moreau is so sexy, the whereabouts of Ian Nash's MS, Josh's incredibly smelly socks, the 1990 Federal election, whether it's time now for a coffee, sorrow as one's kids mature, some good Donald Friend pictures—and some crude ones, why Toby's shoes are at the hearth downstairs, elastic bands, Paul Muldoon, whether to plant out the tiny pink hawthorn, relation between soul and accident, being and becoming, calling people size-nicknames, the Angry Penguins, pleasures of drinking cheap brut, Schubert's unfinished symphony, buying a pair of insoles and some new Bic shavers, giving Casper his dinner, must get more petrol tomorrow, must go on tidying papers, write to Next Door about the ivy on our wall, Josh wanting some small change, the violin as a cultural artefact, blackberry jam, unwrapping those Vienna frankfurters, getting one sock damp as a result of going out into the garden without shoes, time to ring Georgia, also the Prideaux, rewinding the video, whether there's a meeting on Monday, a cup of instant coffee, washing all the whites, Hilary McPhee's agenda, *New Yorker* cartoons, casalinga bread with cheese, replying to Xmas parties in different outfits or departments, spiders, time for a shower in the morning, not remembering my dreams the last few days, vegetable omelette, the Albigensians, how to make coconut rice properly, transferring the cherries from plastic bag to bowl for better keeping, old Alex Craig, the bills being pretty much up to date for the nonce, the Bosnian serbs, a Jaguar I saw in Princes Street today flying a huge Croatian flag, watering the ferns, reasons why I can't read in bed— not for long anyway, why John Brumby isn't more impressive, the boys coming home suddenly with a new Vietnamese friend called Charles, bark paintings and the 'jelly baby' figure who is *not* one of the Lightning Brothers, driving on a sunny morning through Malvern and Tooronga, a prickly feeling in my right big toe, Brett Whiteley's peculiarly intense interest in women's bums, Ubud, geography quizzes with the boys, Guinness, schoolbook-swapping day, Hope's 'Pseododoxia Epidemice' and Iris Murdoch's *The Sea, The Sea*. And so, that was one, plural way of looking at Saturday, 25 November, it being a mild, moonless night now.

WET GHOST

The old horse, it was,
fell dead, slid into the dam,
where it floated, still as can be,
shaped like a European country
for months on end.

Ducks perched on top of it,
brilliant green weed
bearded the muzzle
of its brown persistence,
immovable horse.

Neither gunshots nor the gradual
could abolish
that weird organic island:
it underwrote god
as a comic author

but one day it simply drifted ashore
then fell to bits
in the normal way.

YABBYING

for Joshua

Under a snood of mizzling cloud
blackwoods are glowering greenly down
into the water's torpid mirror.

Everything here is more
or less as leisurely and primaeval
as the underheard forest-tops

moaning before a lofty salt wind.
And it's going to take human patience
to wait wet above the knotted meat

and then draw living creatures in
little by little, sliding a butterfly-net
under them, terribly gentle

till, plop, they go into a bucket.
But we're every bit as tardy
as Mother Nature laying down, year after year,

her pavlova of limestone
or hoisting skyward great eucalypts
in a world that has no name at all for us.

EARLY ON WITH SMOG

Vinyl street, cherry-red cars, the dusty shops TO LET
that's life this morning,
                    genuine like hay fever.
The rule of local shitheads marches on,
suggesting 'Land of Hope and Glory'
                    done with gumleaves on the Mall
by pimply Year Nine students, minorly tattooed.
Even the kerbside plane trees are acting rheumatic.
Pure beef are the frontpage faces, damp and red,
                    fit for a boardroom trauma,
but Missus Roofless trudges from the park,
her dressing-gown done up with binder twine,
gear in a plastic roll.

The economy she lives in (barely)
is not capable of care because
money can only measure surfaces,
marrying nothing but itself.

These are the bone-dry years of qualified hate.

Why do the 90s townhouse draughtsmen
primp little pediments on top of everything
or green-and-salmon lattice? To what end?
This is material drearsville, pretty much
late in civilization's dreck and text,
                    the macworld only offering
some Turkish Humphrey Bogart padding by
like Heraclitus in a mackintosh.

And what in fact might his hopes be,
at the wrong end of a century?

THE DEFICIT SUCKS

Sniff. So life has played itself out,
first as tragedy, then as theme park
since we all have something smart to sell.

Sado-monetarism is hard to fit
into a poem, but I'd say by now
that we all know roughly what it means

at the dag-end of this millennium.
At worst, your pessimist might say
(of course, that's why they're pessimists)

that healthy government by the rich
of the rich and for the rich
will never pass away. Like fleas

or the common cold. Therefore
we'll flog our universities
to golden boys from overseas,

dumping all scholarship that doesn't pay
in the polluted waters of
Sydney Harbour or Port Phillip Bay.

THE AUTUMN KNOT

What is it you were wanting
  When wishes were king?
You've got what you asked for,
  But wanted the wrong thing.

MORE LOSS

It is over:
         having been
a slice or continuing slab of your life
which, along with
                  big surf and yellow sand

was going
         to be forever.
Gumleaves. Cloud. Shelves of rock.

Where has the green past
                  washed away to?
Can it be
         in some landscaped part
of the cerebellum

or just floating out there
                  insubstantial
         in the heartless blue ether?

God allegedly knows.

THE GLORY

It was only a narrow grainy sandbar
allegedly the isthmus of Panama
as I walked barefoot
               between two oceans
the lucid Atlantic trickling over
from left to right, prettily rippling
into a receptive green Pacific

As we ambled south the beautiful overflow
deepened and gushed, a liquid jade
becoming torrent, not pleasure,
till all of a sudden the fear took hold of me
that I would never reach South America

The lemonade-coloured water swallowed me
like the end of everything
and suddenly then we were standing together
on a brilliantly final dripping pinnacle
alive or dead
               'Where are we?' I asked you
gasping in all that salty glory
at the blinding end of a lifetime's tether
'This is Nirvana,' you replied

We had left the terrible world behind

OXFORD POETS

Fleur Adcock
Moniza Alvi
Joseph Brodsky
Basil Bunting
Tessa Rose Chester
Daniela Crăsnaru
Greg Delanty
Michael Donaghy
Keith Douglas
D. J. Enright
Roy Fisher
Ida Affleck Graves
Ivor Gurney
David Harsent
Gwen Harwood
Anthony Hecht
Zbigniew Herbert
Tobias Hill
Thomas Kinsella
Brad Leithauser
Derek Mahon
Jamie McKendrick

Sean O'Brien
Alice Oswald
Peter Porter
Craig Raine
Zsuzsa Rakovszky
Christopher Reid
Stephen Romer
Eva Salzman
Carole Satyamurti
Peter Scupham
Jo Shapcott
Penelope Shuttle
Goran Simić
Anne Stevenson
George Szirtes
Grete Tartler
Edward Thomas
Charles Tomlinson
Marina Tsvetaeva
Chris Wallace-Crabbe
Hugo Williams

WILL YE NO' COME BACK AGAIN?

Music talks directly to the gods,
its marrow somewhere far to the north of meaning,
like a spectral dog at the end of your backyard,
not where it's really at,
                        in a material form.

The *Jahrzeit* burns down yellow and low.
They will not come back again;
yet music glides in under the rooftree
and yearningly plunders the past.

It can turn your poor heart over
or simply touch the skies
                        with a dry finger.
A trumpet flares, or a liquorice clarinet;
the piano creeps in under your second skin;
and the dead are suddenly walking
through our pale bodies
like frost or influenza,

enabled all of a sudden, wet with tears,
plucked out of limbo, purely because
our music spoke directly to the gods.

Black, squealing cockatoos chew on our pinecones
but there was a time
when some visiting priest
would say mass
at a ruined house by the creek,
bespeaking Presence.

Steadily, big waves are thumping on the sand.

TOWNSHIP, WITH CURRAWONGS

Upright, courtly, maker of knives,
the local handyman is dead
                    and gone from his roadbend,
he who drank away
fourteen blocks of land.

Plumbers and sturdy electricians
can be got pretty cheap round here,
as long as the surf isn't up and rolling:
first things first.

Nobody fells tall timber
from these bird-crowded slopes now
but the feral blackberries
make wonderful jam.

The angles of the hills compose tangentially.

Rabbits on a rampage
have dug odd holes in the turf
of this undulating tennis court;
you have to fossick for the yellow balls
in giant hedge or glossy shrub.
You crawl under hydrangeas.

Splendidly wise, the bowerbirds come back
when they know holidays are blown away,
the fibro cottages empty.

There's also the practical man who gave
his missus a mower for Christmas,
and all that lush grass to be levelled
in regular swathes.

A PALGRAVE

for Jacky Simms

Pocketsized in Oxford blue, printed on
wartime rice-paper, this was the book
I gave my mother in 1947
for her birthday, the fortieth, her second
after Dad flew home from the Japanese war.
A clutch of poetry!
      I was only twelve
but would be rounding thirteen the following day.
Just then, at the tempting newsagents', I must
have caught a glimpse of where my future lay
patterned in those rectangles of type,
apotropaic like midnight acorns
and memorable as a Christmas carol.

Just look: a dull small navyblue volume
as full of tricks as a marvellous Jack-in-the-Box
furnished me forth with Flecker, Keats and Marvell,
and, yet more wondrous, with 'Byzantium'
or Empson's cubist version of a view
and the suasive charms of urban Louis Macneice.
Back there, I swam through Mother's looking-glass
which gave onto the modern, its reality
(however sombre the black print on the page)
ever so much more real than life itself.
Ah, poetry, the siren on the rocks.